Little Kids Can Write Books Too!

Making Classroom Books with Young Children

by
Diane Bonica

illustrated by Veronica Terrill

Cover by Veronica Terrill

Copyright © 1994, Good Apple

ISBN No. 0-86653-784-8

Printing No. 98

Good Apple
A Division of Frank Schaffer Publications, Inc.
23740 Hawthorne Boulevard
Torrance, CA 90505-5927

D0865600

A Special Thank-You

To All My Students at Living Savior Preschool

Dedication

This book is dedicated to Ashley Emma and all young children who wish to become authors!

GA1478

Table of Contents

Foreword

Nothing draws young children to reading more than hearing their own stories read. Whenever I begin a class-written book in my busy preschool room, it acts as a magnet and draws children from all corners. The students feel ownership in the words, and they delight in the story and its familiar repetition.

Nothing is more joyful than sharing this type of personal literature with young learners, but until now no other task has been as time-consuming for teachers. This book ends the drudgery of assembling class books! It provides you with all your class needs to create twenty student-written volumes. Each book may be a project for the entire class or it can be done in a small group. When the writing and illustrating are complete, all pages fit neatly inside a file folder cover. The books can be secured with plastic rings or brads, and then they are ready for lots of reading and sharing.

Try one of these books and you and your students will be hooked! The children will ask to make books over and over. Beginning readers will choose the class-made volumes as practice reading material. Your students will have great pride in the stories that they have created. You will have great success as bookbinder and story facilitator!

GA1478

Introduction

Little Kids Can Write Books Too! includes:

- Specific instructions for twenty class books

- Author pages

- Artistically designed book covers

- Writing process directions

- Illustration ideas and materials

- A selection of books to help teach curriculum skills as well as writing skills

GA1478

Book Assembly

 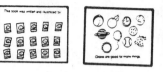 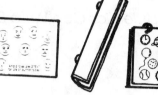

File Folder	Illustrated Cover (glue on folder)	Author Page	Front Page	Student Pages	Final Page	Three-Hole Punch	Done

Step One: Read teacher instructions for each book.

Step Two: Color the illustrated cover.
Glue it to the front of a file folder.
Cover the folder with clear Con-Tact™ paper or laminate it.

Step Three: Assemble the author page.

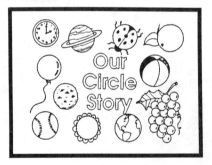

Step Four: Complete the front page.

Circles are good for many things.

Step Five: Add illustrated student book pages.
Allow one page per child. (Reproduce as many as you need.)

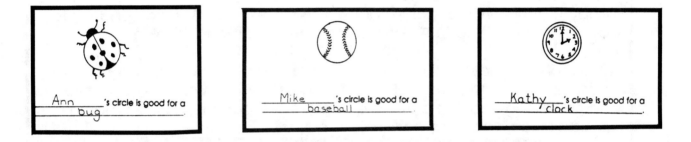

Ann's circle is good for a bug

Mike's circle is good for a baseball

Kathy's circle is good for a clock

Step Six: Add the final story page. (In some instances, students' photos may be used on this page also.)

And circles are GREAT for lots of author faces!

Step Seven: With a three-hole punch, make holes in pages and cover. Secure with brads or plastic rings.

GA1478

Author Photos

Personal authorship is very rewarding for young children, and providing a visual credit in each book is even more satisfying. The following Author Page will help you create a photographic credit page to use with each book your class creates.

Take pictures of each of your students. If you have a 35-mm camera you may take up to three children in each photo. Process the film and cut out small photos of each child measuring 2" x 1¹/₂" (5.08 x 3.79 cm). Glue the photos on the form on the next page and write each author's name under each picture. You can make several copies of this form on your copy machine. Color copies are great but expensive. Black and white copies come out perfectly on the light setting of most machines.

These photos may be used on the author page of each book, and they can also be cut up and placed on the story line where each child's name belongs. Having a photo on each book page helps the children in a class to learn one another's names quickly.

GA1478

Author Page

GA1478

This book was written and illustrated by:

Our Circle Story
A Shape and Adjective Book

_____'s circle is good for a
silly clown   .

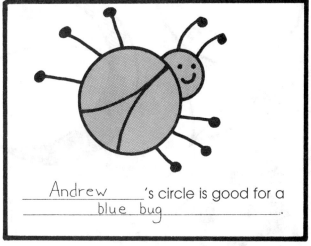

Andrew_____'s circle is good for a
blue bug   .

Writing and Illustrating

Prewrite: Conduct a circle shape search in your class or schoolyard. Share all the circle items you find.

Get Set: Draw circles on a chart or chalkboard. Ask the children to help add details to change a circle into a sun, a ball, a watch, etc.

Word Play: Brainstorm lots of circle items and their one-word descriptions. A watch could be quiet, a ball could be bouncy, and a sun could be big.

Illustrate: Give each child a book page and a 3" (7.62 cm) circle of colored paper. Glue the circle to the book page, and invite each child to sketch in details to invent a circle item.

Capture the Story: Move from child to child jotting down each contribution. A finished example might be, "Andrew's circle is good for a blue bug."

The Final Page: The last page of this book requires a small circular photo of each student. Directions for making class pictures are found on page viii. Randomly glue circle photos to this final page.

GA1478

Circles are good for many things.

's circle is good for a _____ .

And circles are GREAT for lots of author faces!

The Very Hungry Caterpillar
Our Version Based on Eric Carle's Book

He ate _____ Amy _____ 's
_____ birthday cake _____ .

He ate _____ Jim _____ 's
_____ ice-cream cone _____ .

Writing and Illustrating

Prewrite: Read the book *The Very Hungry Caterpillar* by Eric Carle. Delight in the story and do lots of talking about foods that are fun to eat.

Get Set: Provide your students with magazines, and let them cut out pictures of food.

Word Play: Ask the children to choose one food picture to share with the class. Take turns describing how each food looks or tastes. A lemon might be "juicy" or "yellow," while ice cream might be "cold" and "nutty."

Illustrate: Pass out the book pages. Ask the students to glue their food pictures to the pages. Give each child four or five colored dot stickers to create a caterpillar on the same page. Use markers or crayons for the caterpillar details.

Capture the Story: As the illustrations are completed, ask each child for the story line. One example might be, "He ate Ashley's birthday cake."

The Final Page: The last page of this book needs one or several butterflies. You might use stickers, photos, or child-drawn illustrations.

GA1478

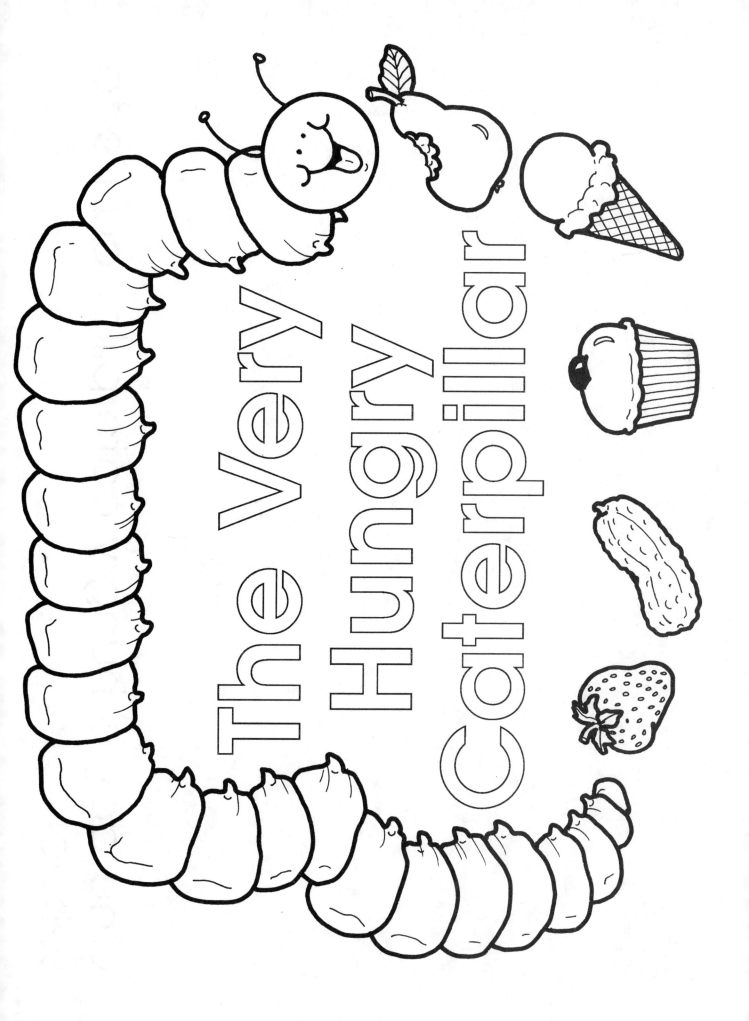

The Very Hungry Caterpillar

One day a hungry caterpillar came to school . . .

He ate _____'s _____.

Eating so much much made the caterpillar tired. He built a cocoon and went to sleep. When he woke up, he was not a caterpillar. He had turned into a big, bright BUTTERFLY!

Find the Pumpkin
A Lift-the-Flap Book

Writing and Illustrating

Prewrite: Stage a pumpkin hunt in your class. Hide candy pumpkins around your room. Ask children to hunt until they find one pumpkin.

Get Set: Regroup and talk about the locations of the little pumpkins. One might have been under the chair or another might have been on the bookshelf.

Word Play: Cut several 4" x 6" (10.16 x 15.24 cm) pictures from magazines. The pictures should represent possible hiding places, like doors, windows, shelves, chairs, etc. Reinforce the magazine items by gluing them to white paper and cutting them out again. Tape one side of the picture to each book page for a lift-the-flap book. Brainstorm many location statements for each picture. If the picture is a chair, your pumpkin could be hiding around it, behind it, under it, etc.

Illustrate: Pass out 3" x 5" (7.62 x 12.7 cm) sheets of white paper and ask each child to draw a pumpkin. Cut out each drawing and glue it behind one of the magazine pictures.

Capture the Story: The students will give a location phrase for each pumpkin's hiding place. Jot each response on the book page. A finished example might read, "Who put a pumpkin behind the clock?" Next to the pumpkin illustration write "Adam did."

The Final Page: Complete this page with some additional child-drawn Halloween items.

GA1478

Find the Pumpkin

Where did the children hide their pumpkins? Let's go look!

Who put a pumpkin _____ ?

We found them all!
HAPPY HALLOWEEN!

A-Hunting We Will Go
Our Version Based on John Langstaff's Book

A-hunting we will go.
A-hunting we will go.
___Joe___ will catch a ___fox___,
And put it ___in___ a ___box___,
And then we'll let it go.

A-hunting we will go.
A-hunting we will go.
___Sue___ will catch a ___bug___,
And put it ___in___ a ___rug___,
And then we'll let it go.

Writing and Illustrating

Prewrite: Read the book *A-Hunting We Will Go* by John Langstaff. The children will catch on to the patterned writing very quickly. Let them predict where each animal will be placed and then read the text.

Get Set: Read the book again and again, and give alternate solutions to the ones offered by Mr. Langstaff.

Word Play: Brainstorm other animals and possible resting places. Play with lots of rhymes. Catch a bee and put him in a tree, catch a sheep and put him in a Jeep™, or catch a mallard and put him in a salad.

Illustrate: Distribute book pages and provide magazine pictures of several different animals. Older students might prefer to draw their own animals. With an animal glued or drawn on the book page, ask each child to illustrate the location.

Capture the Story: As the artwork progresses, copy down each author's rhyme. An example of a finished page might be:
    A-hunting we will go.
    A-hunting we will go.
    Susan will catch a mouse.
    And put him in a house.
    And then we'll let him go.

The Final Page: Glue additional magazine animals to this page or have students draw animals to illustrate it.

GA1478

We're going hunting, so let's all sing. . .

A-hunting we will go.
A-hunting we will go.
We will catch a _____
And put it _____ a _____
And then we'll let it go.

A-hunting we will go.
A-hunting we will go.
We'll make believe,
But before we leave,
We'll always let them go!

Thankful We
A Handy Book for Thanksgiving

(four different colors)

(brown)

Becky 's hand gives thanks for her mom. She's nice.

Tami 's hand gives thanks for flowers. They're pretty.

Writing and Illustrating

Prewrite: Fill a cornucopia or basket with small toys or items, such as a house, a car, a doll family, a dog, a cat, a bird, a school, etc. Pull one item out at a time and tell a thankful tale. You might say, "I'm thankful for birds because they sing."

Get Set: Brainstorm with the class for several other things to be thankful for. It may help to brainstorm in the categories of people, places, animals, or things. Allow time for each child to have a turn.

Word Play: List many reasons to be thankful for each item or person. "We are thankful for food because it tastes good, it is good for us, and it fills up hungry tummies."

Illustrate: Paint hand turkeys for illustrations. Paint the thumb and palm of each child's hand brown; paint each finger a different color. Press the painted hands onto the book pages. When the paint is dry, add beaks, feet, and eyes with markers.

Capture the Story: Copy each child's thankful tale onto the book page. A finished page might read, "Becky's hand gives thanks for her mom. She's nice."

The Final Page: Illustrate this page with Thanksgiving stickers or individual drawings by students.

GA1478

Little turkey hands have we.
They are thankful as can be.
Read our story and you'll see.

_____'s hand gives thanks for _____.

Counting blessings is such fun.
We hope you read every one.
HAPPY
THANKSGIVING!

Our Hungry Thing
Our Version Based on Slepian and Seidler's Book

He asked for some ____pilk____, so ____Tim____ gave him some ___milk___.

He asked for some ___sapples___. So ____Mike____ gave him some ___apples___.

Writing and Illustrating

Prewrite: Read the book *The Hungry Thing* by Jan Slepian and Ann Seidler. Share the fun of this unique story and get involved with the nonsense rhyming.

Get Set: Play with nonsensical rhyme. Change each child's name to a nonsense word. "Nancy is Dancy, Ruth is Guth, and Marco is Parco."

Word Play: Let each child make up a silly food rhyme and have the rest of the children guess what it is. You might like to structure the guessing game with the phrase, "I want _____ for dinner." Fill in the blank with a silly food rhyme. "Hoop" would work for "soup." "Tice" would work for "rice."

Illustrate: Using crayons or markers, ask the children to draw a hungry thing monster on a book page. On the same page have each author sketch and color the item that the monster wishes to eat. Younger preschoolers might be more comfortable with magazine food pictures.

Capture the Story: Record each child's contribution to the story. A finished page might be "He asked for some harrots. So Lindsey gave him some carrots."

The Final Page: Ask the children to draw one hungry monster around the words on the last page. Color it with crayons or markers.

GA1478

One day, a Hungry Thing came to _____ School.

He asked for some _____, so _____ gave him some _____.

Then he was full and he said, "Thank you!"

December Colors
A Book of Holiday Hues

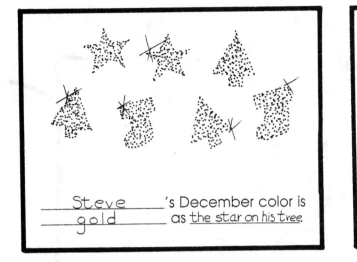

_____Steve_____ 's December color is
_____gold_____ as <u>the star on his tree</u>.

_____Karen_____ 's December color is
_____black_____ as <u>Santa's boots</u>.

Writing and Illustrating

Prewrite: Play a holiday I Spy game. Begin with examples like "I spy something green. It hangs on your front door. I spy something red. It is round. It hangs on your tree. It has a hook."

Get Set: Make a color list on the chalkboard or on a chart. Ask children to suggest holiday colors. Brainstorm items for each color. Brown could be reindeer, dreidels, pinecones, etc. Yellow could be candle flames, stars, lights, angel wings, etc.

Word Play: Ask the children to select a color and an item to match. Now ask for details. Black could be for soot. Where? On Santa's boot.

Illustrate: Use holiday cutout sponge shapes to decorate each book page. The author will paint in the color of his or her story. A child whose December color is blue will paint all blue holiday shapes.

Capture the Story: You may choose to write down the story lines before the painting is done. A finished story could be "Marion's December color is gold as the star on the top of her tree."

The Final Page: Add sponge shapes in all colors to this page. It will be most festive!

GA1478

December
Colors

Colors, colors everywhere,
Paint winter with a holiday flair!

_____'s December color is _____

as _____.

What a colorful month! Happy Holidays!

Guess the Gift
A First Book of Riddles

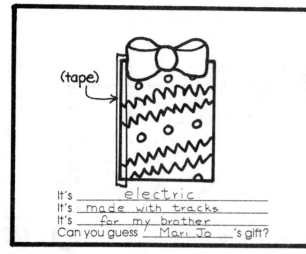

It's ___electric___
It's ___made with tracks___
It's ___for my brother___
Can you guess ___Mari Jo___'s gift?

(tape)

(lift)

(magazine picture)

(back side of gift)

It's a train!

(teacher writes this)

It's ___electric___
It's ___made with tracks___
It's ___for my brother___
Can you guess ___Mari Jo___'s gift?

Writing and Illustrating

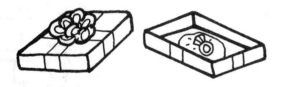

Prewrite: Wrap four or five small box lids in holiday paper. Glue a picture of a gift item inside the bottom of each box. Show the gift to your children. Tell them that they can guess what the present is. Give good descriptive hints for each box. You might say, "It's round. It's shiny. It's for a girl or mom. It's for her finger." Of course, it's a ring!

Get Set: Provide lots of magazines; store catalogs are the best. Have your class holiday-shop with scissors. Ask each child to cut out a gift item.

Word Play: With items hidden behind their backs, let the children create their own riddles. Even young four-year-olds can succeed at this task. The process is fun, and it is an excellent language builder.

Illustrate: Hand out 4" x 6" (10.16 x 15.24 cm) pieces of colored paper and ask the children to design their own holiday boxes. Glue precut paper bows to the packages. Tape the packages to the book pages on one side only for a lift-the-flap story. Glue a picture of a gift under each present.

Capture the Story: Record the riddles on each author's page. A finished riddle could be, "It's electric. It's made with tracks. It's for my brother. Can you guess Mari Jo's gift?"

The Final Page: Add more packages to the last page. They can be cut out, or simple drawings can be made.

GA1478

The children in _____
School have done lots of shopping.
Can you guess the gifts?

It's _____

It's _____

It's _____

Can you guess _____'s gift?

You're done!
Wasn't unwrapping fun?

Snowflake Action
A Book Using Verbs and Similes

_____Jane_____'s snowflakes ___drop___
like_____bouncy balls_____.

_____'s snowflakes ___twirl___
like____white umbrellas____.

Writing and Illustrating

Prewrite: Play the "Waltz of the Snowflakes" from the *Nutcracker Suite* and let your students dance as snow ballerinas. You will need a large space like a gym or multipurpose room. When the children are dancing, point out different movements–Brian bends, Sally skips, Nathan tiptoes, etc.

Get Set: Return to class and talk about all the ways that the dancers moved. Take each movement and brainstorm all other people or things that move that way. Snowflakes twirl like tops, dancers, umbrellas, merry-go-rounds, etc.

Word Play: Ask each child to select a movement and perform it for the class. The other students guess the movement and then name other things that move the same way. Jack could jump and so do kids on a trampoline, parachutists, and grasshoppers.

Illustrate: Use premade stamps or sponge shapes to paint snowflakes on the book pages. Add a bit of blue to the white paint so that the snowflakes will be visible on white paper.

Capture the Story: Ask each child for a movement and someone that moves that way. A completed story line might read, "Jenna's snowflakes drop like bouncing balls."

The Final Page: Paint additional snowflakes on this page. Overlapping will create a "storm" scene.

GA1478

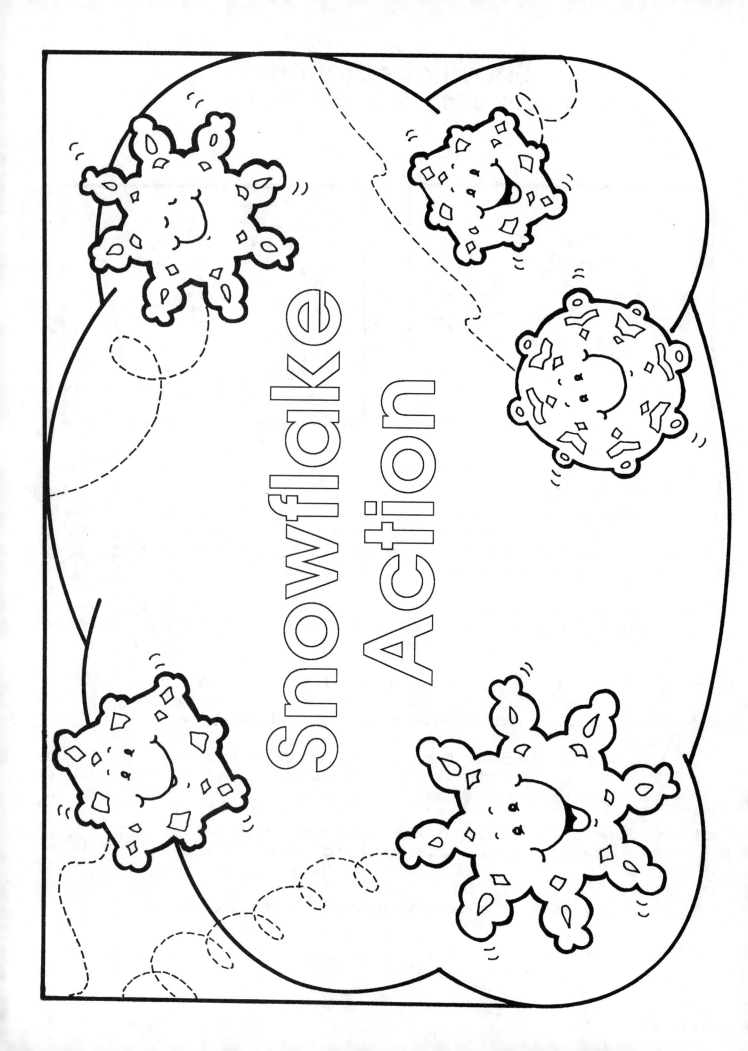

Snowflake Action

Snowflakes are falling at
School. Watch the dance!

_____'s snowflakes

like _____ .

Wow! Snowflakes move in many ways.

Mary Wore Her Red Dress
Our Version Based on the Book by Merle Peek

(author photo)

(magazine outfit)

_____Bob_____ wore _his 49er shirt_,
his 49er shirt , _his 49er shirt_ ,
_____Bob_____ wore _his 49er shirt_
all winter long.

_____Mark_____ wore _his leather jacket_,
his leather jacket , _his leather jacket_.
_____Mark_____ wore _his leather jacket_
all winter long.

Writing and Illustrating

Prewrite: Read the book *Mary Wore Her Red Dress* by Merle Peek. This is a fun story in patterned rhyme. It is about several animals getting dressed up to go to a birthday party.

Get Set: Provide several children's clothing catalogs and ask each child to cut out a complete outfit. Younger students may need assistance with this task. When the outfits are cut out, replace the head of each catalog model with a small photo you have taken of each child.

Word Play: Sing the song that this story was based on. The words and music are at the back of Mr. Peek's book. Ask the children to add new verses using the clothing that they cut out of the catalog.

Illustrate: Glue the new outfit and the student's photo to the book page. Be ready for laughter as each child views himself or herself in a different outfit. Students might like to add an illustrated background, but it is not required.

Capture the Story: This is the easiest story to record. Each child will simply state what the new outfit is. A finished story could be "Joel wore his leather coat, leather coat, leather coat. Joel wore his leather coat all winter long."

The Final Page: Glue additional outfits to the final page in a collage style.

GA1478

Mary Wore Her Red Dress

Mary wore her red dress,
red dress, red dress.
Mary wore her red dress
all winter long. AND . . .

_____ wore _____,

_____ wore _____

_____ all winter long.

We all liked dressing up,
dressing up, dressing up.
We all liked dressing up,
all winter long!

A Friendship Book
Based on the Book by Joan Walsh Anglund

_____Kim_____'s friend is someone who
invites her to lunch_____.
_____Kim_____'s friend is someone like
_____Linda_____.

_____Tom_____'s friend is someone who
plays Ninja Turtles_____.
_____Tom_____'s friend is someone like
_____Joey_____.

Writing and Illustrating

Prewrite: Read Joan Walsh Anglund's book *A Friend Is Someone Who Likes You*. Your students will be able to offer other friendship definitions.

Get Set: Talk about friends and the activities they do together.

Word Play: Brainstorm all the activities that children do with a friend. A favorite response is *play*, but this term is too broad, so let your students break it down into types of play. Friends play checkers, games, hide-and-seek, house, school, and much more.

Illustrate: On the book page, each student will draw a self-portrait and one of a friend. Use markers, crayons, or colored pencils to complete the drawings. Younger preschoolers might like to fill in features on pre-made paper doll shapes. Each method will be effective.

Capture the Story: As the drawings are completed, record each special friendship story. A final product might read, "Jill's friend is someone who invites her to lunch. Jill's friend is someone like Linda."

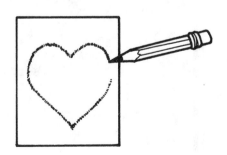

The Final Page: Draw a large heart around the words on this page. Paste your author pictures inside the heart.

GA1478

A Friendship Book

A friend is someone who likes you.
A friend is someone like You!
And . . . .

_____'s friend is someone who

_____.

_____'s friend is someone like

_____.

Friends are people who like you.
We are happy for friends.

We Love You More
A First Book of Comparisons

_____ loves you more than
bees love honey.

___Sarah___ loves you more than
mommies love babies.

Writing and Illustrating

Prewrite: Children love to exaggerate. This book is sure to please them. Begin by talking about favorite things. Mrs. Johnson loves tacos, grandchildren, and storybooks. Invite the children to list their favorite things.

Get Set: Move from personal favorite items to the favorite objects of animals and things. This is an exciting thinking activity and one that will produce many smiles. Dogs love bones best, or is it slippers? Monkeys love bananas and climbing trees. Pencils love sharp points. Dentists love fillings.

Word Play: Ask each student to cut out an object or animal from a magazine. Share the photos and brainstorm favorite things. Teddy bears love hugs. Brushes love paints.

Illustrate: Glue the magazine items to the book pages and ask each child to draw the favorite thing on the same page. The child who chooses a kitten might draw a ball of yarn, etc. You will need markers and crayons for this activity.

Capture the Story: These story lines are pure fun. Copy each child's contribution onto the book page. A completed line might read, "Jonathan loves you more than bees love honey."

The Final Page: Decorate this page with heart cutouts or valentine stickers. Have fun!

56

GA1478

We love you more,
That's for sure!
Read and find out how.

_____ loves you more than _____

_____ love _____ .

See,
we do love you
MORE!

Dear Zoo
Our Version Based on Rod Campbell's Book

He was too ___scary___
We sent him back.
So they sent us a . . . .

He was too ___scary___
We sent him back.
So they sent us a . . . .

Writing and Illustrating

Prewrite: Read Rod Campbell's book *Dear Zoo*. This lift-the-flap story is a great treat for early learners.

Get Set: A trip to a zoo would be the perfect follow-up to this story.

Word Play: Brainstorm all kinds of zoo animals. Try to come up with a different animal for each child. Brainstorm why each of these animals would be inappropriate as a class pet. A lion would be too noisy, a hippopotamus too big, etc.

Illustrate: Hand out colored construction paper and ask each student to design a shipping crate for the animal. On the book page, ask each child to draw his or her animal. Cut out the crate and tape it over the animal drawing. Tape only one side so that you can lift the flap.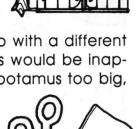

Capture the Story: As the animals are crated for delivery, record each child's story. A finished page about a snake might read, "He was too scary. We sent him back. So they sent us a . . . ."

The Final Page: Brainstorm what the perfect class pet would be and draw a picture of it on this page. If you already have a resident animal, a photo would be excellent.

GA1478

We wrote to the zoo to send us a class pet. They sent us a . . . .

He was too _____ .

We sent him back.

So they sent us a . . . .

He was just right!
So we kept him.

Growing Up
A First Book About Careers

When _____Ted_____ grows up,
___he___ 's going to be a draftsman
so __he__ can __draw buildings__ .

When _____Debbie_____ grows up,
___she___ 's going to be a _writer_
so __she__ can __write books__ .

Writing and Illustrating

Prewrite: Make a deck of career cards or buy a commercially developed set. Share the cards with your students and talk about the work that each person does.

Get Set: Make a simple map of your community. Use paper dol cutouts and place workers in each town building. Shopkeepers, doctors, vets, hairdressers, pastors, teachers, and bankers will all have a place.

Word Play: Brainstorm other careers that are not mentioned. The children might have relatives in out-of-the-ordinary jobs; always mention what work is done by each worker.

Illustrate: Using the author photos, ask your students to draw themselves in career clothing. Younger children might like to use the pictures of career people from coloring books. Their photos will be placed in the head position.

Capture the Story: The stories in this book are longer than the others have been but easy to write with good brainstorming. A finished page could read, "When Ronnie grows up, he's going to be a draftsman so he can draw plans for buildings."

The Final Page: Draw a globe around the print on this page. Have the children color it with markers.

GA1478

When we grow up,
We'll do many things.
Read and find out
What we'll be.

When _____ grows up,

_____ 's going to be a _____

can _____ so _____ .

What a wonderful
world it will be!

April Rain
A Book Using Action Words

___Mary___ 's April rain <u>squish-squashes</u> on <u>flower petals</u>.

___Jill___ 's April rain ___runs___ on <u>the car windows</u>.

Writing and Illustrating

Prewrite: Run outside on a rainy day and spend a minute or two between the raindrops. Return to class and talk about the experience.

Get Set: Listen to the Disney record "April Showers" or watch this segment from the movie *Bambi*. This delightful rain sequence will help with brainstorming.

Word Play: Brainstorm all the noisy ways that rain falls. It could drip, splatter, splash, dance, tiptoe, etc. Talk about where the wet drops rest: in your eyes, on the window, on the rooftops, under the tree, etc.

Illustrate: Using eyedroppers, ask each child to place a row of colored drops of paint across the top of the book page. When the row of drops is complete, hold the paper upright and let the paint drop like rain down the paper. Allow for drying time.

Capture the Story: When the colorful paintings are complete, copy the noisy stories on the pages. A finished page might read "Holly's April rain squish-squashes on flower petals."

The Final Page: Ask each child to make a colorful drop on this page—a painted fingerprint would be perfect! When the paint is dry, transform each drip into a musical note.

GA1478

April Rain

on _____ 's April rain
_____.

April rain dances to school.
Can you hear it?

What lovely music
is the
APRIL RAIN!

A Dinosaur's Walk
A Book About Position

(stamp)   (drawing)

She went __behind__ the ___tree___.

She went __under__ the __bridge__.

Writing and Illustrating

Prewrite: Set up an obstacle course in your class or gym. Provide lots of opportunities for your students to do many movements–things to go over, under, around, behind, between, and through.

Get Set: Play on the obstacle course and talk a lot about where each child is. Peter is on top of the steps; Matt is under the blanket; Diana is up the ladder; and Kaley is on the rope.

Word Play: Take a mental walk through your school surroundings. This could be similar to the adventure taken in the book *Going on a Bear Hunt* by John Burningham. Remember to go around the flagpole, under the swings, through the tunnel, across the grass, etc.

Illustrate: Purchase a dinosaur stamp or dinosaur stickers so that the illustration of the book's main character will be the same on all book pages. Ask the children to draw the location pictures and then stamp Debbie the Dinosaur in place. If Debbie is going up the hill in the child's story, he or she will draw the hill and then stamp Debbie on the way up.

Capture the Story: Each child will simply tell you where the dinosaur is. A completed page might be "She went behind the tree."

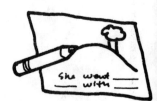

The Final Page: Draw a roof and walls around the text on this page. The drawing will represent a school building. Paste individual author photos inside the drawing and stamp Debbie there too!

GA1478

She went _____ the _____ .

She got back to school
just in time for a
SNACK!

The May Bugs
Based on David Cleveland's book *April Rabbits*

On the ___7th___ day of May _Kathy_ saw _seven_ bugs _playing instruments_.

On the ___2nd___ day of May _____ saw _two_ bugs _playing checkers_.

Writing and Illustrating

Prewrite: Read David Cleveland's book *April Rabbits*. As you read, begin to guess what the rabbits might be doing each day.

Get Set: Play a pantomime game. Each child will demonstrate a motion and the other students will guess what it is. You may wish to model a few at first—jumping rope, skating, hopscotching, bike riding, etc.

Word Play: Mr. Cleveland's book ends with a perfect suggestion for a May story—"Hippos." Unfortunately, hippos are not easy for preschoolers to draw so we opted for bugs instead. Brainstorm all the actions that your bugs will be doing in May. Your pantomime game should have given your students many ideas.

Illustrate: An easy bug illustration is made with a painted fingerprint and details shown with a marker. The child with May 2 makes two fingerprints while the child with May 21 makes twenty-one. Use markers or crayons to add the motion details.

Capture the Story: Move from author to author recording this fun book. A finished page might read, "On the 7th day of May, Scott saw seven bugs playing instruments."

The Final Page: Ask each child to draw a bug reading a book for this page. Notice that it is not necessary to have thirty-one pages of text. This last page will take care of any leftover May days.

GA1478

The May Bugs

On the first day of May, the children at School saw one bug

resting on a sunny flower.

On the _____ day of May

saw _____ bugs

_____ .

On the last day of May,
many bugs came to school
and learned how to read!

We Are Readers
A Book to Celebrate Learning to Read

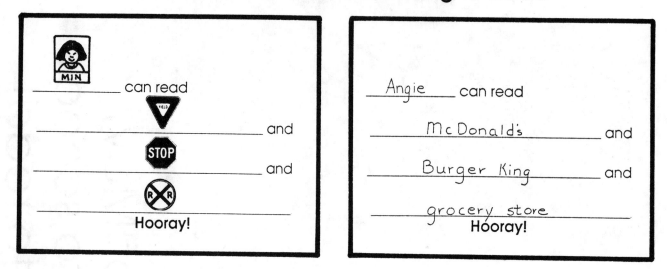

Writing and Illustrating

Prewrite: Cut out visually recognizable print from newspapers and magazines and display it on a chart for your students. Advertising symbols from McDonald's and Burger King™ are perfect examples. Try to find symbols that have both logos and print. Another great example is a stop sign.

Get Set: Let students hunt through newspapers and magazines to find three or four examples that they can recognize.

Word Play: Share at least one choice from each student. See how many other students can read it too. Preschoolers who never gave a thought to being able to read love this book activity. You might challenge older primary students to include some "just print" along with a symbol example.

Illustrate: The magazine and newspaper cutouts are the illustrations for this book. Just glue them on the lines provided.

Capture the Story: Illustrating this book completes the story! The words and pictures are each child's contribution to the book. With older primary children you might like to use two magazine examples and one that is written in by the student.

The Final Page: Paste additional words and symbols on this page.

GA1478

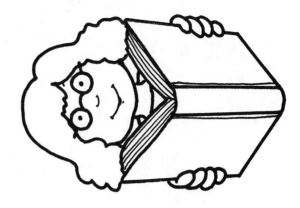
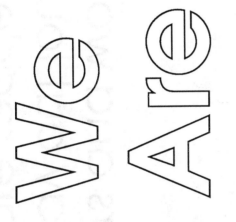

We Are Readers

Letters and words
We say out loud.
We are readers,
And we are **PROUD**.

can read

and

and

Hooray!

Words and letters,
Now we know.
We are readers,
Watch us grow!

Sweet Dreams
A Silly Book to Sleep On

JC's   fish   dream of
juicy   worms   .

's   reindeer   dream of
Christmas   .

Writing and Illustrating

Prewrite: Read a version of "Rip Van Winkle" to your students. Ponder about the dreams you might have if you slept for one hundred years. Talk about sweet dreams.

Get Set: Now it is your turn to do some silly thinking. What if cars could dream? What would delight them? New tires, full tanks of gas!

Word Play: Ask each child to select an inanimate object or an animal and brainstorm sweet dreams for it. Pencils would dream of sharp points, houses would dream of new paint, and telephones would dream of long wires.

Illustrate: Using crayons or markers, ask the children to draw their items and their dreams. Fish dream of juicy worms, reindeer dream of Christmas, umbrellas dream of rainstorms, etc.

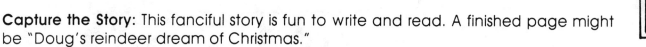

Capture the Story: This fanciful story is fun to write and read. A finished page might be "Doug's reindeer dream of Christmas."

The Final Page: Ask each child to draw a small self-portrait on this page. Eyes closed on all the drawings. We're dreaming!

GA1478

What if things could dream like you
and me?
What would they dream?
Read and see!

dream of _____.

Dreams are fun,
Even silly.
Dream a dream
If you willy!

Quick as a Cricket
Based on the Book by Audrey Wood

Cameron is as hardworking as a beaver.

Alissa is as jumpy as a grasshopper.

Writing and Illustrating

Prewrite: Read Audrey Wood's book, *Quick as a Cricket*. Pay close attention to the patterned writing formula. Enjoy the story and the beautiful illustrations.

Get Set: Brainstorm a list of animals; a deck of animal cards would be helpful. Ask each child to choose a favorite animal. Try to select a different animal for each student.

Word Play: Now it is time for the descriptive work. Brainstorm characteristics for each animal. A lion can be noisy, brave, hairy, etc. Each child will then compare himself or herself with an animal's characteristics.

Illustrate: Ask each child to draw his or her favorite animal on each book page. Markers or crayons are needed here. The students can also add environments for the animals–a sea for fish, a jungle for parrots, etc.

Capture the Story: Comparing yourself to an animal is fun. Copy these story contributions on each book page. A finished page might be "Cameron is as hardworking as a beaver."

The Final Page: Glue a picture of each child to this page.

GA1478

We are quick as crickets.

_____ is

as a _____.

Put them all together,
And you have
US!

Bibliography

Anglund, Joan Walsh, *A Friend Is Someone Who Likes You*, Harcourt, Brace & Jovanovich, 1958.

Burningham, John, *Going on a Bear Hunt*, (Publishing information not available).

Campbell, Rod, *Dear Zoo*, Penguin Books, 1982.

Carle, Eric, *The Very Hungry Caterpillar*, Philomel, 1969.

Cleveland, David, *April Rabbits*, Coward, McCann & Geoghegan, 1978.

Langstaff, John, *A-Hunting We Will Go*, McElderry Books, 1974.

Peek, Merle, *Mary Wore Her Red Dress*, Clarion Books, 1985.

Slepian, Jan and Ann Seidler, *The Hungry Thing*, Scholastic, 1988.

Wood, Audrey, *Quick as a Cricket*, Child's Play Books, 1982.

GA1478